NATIONAL GEOGRAPHIC

First Flight

PIONEER EDITION

By Glen Phelan

CONTENTS

On December 17, 1903, the Wright brothers took off into history!

By Glen Phelan

A strong wind blew over Kitty Hawk, North Carolina. It chilled the air. It blew stinging sand across the beach. Even worse, it might make flying dangerous. Wilbur and Orville Wright hoped the wind would stop.

It didn't. So the two men took a chance. Orville got into the flying machine. He grabbed its controls. The engine rumbled. The plane started to move. Wilbur ran alongside to steady the wings. Then the plane lifted off the ground—and into history!

More than 100 years have passed since this flight. How did the Wright brothers become the first people to fly? This is their story.

Wilbur Wright, 13   *Orville Wright, 9*

Flying Toys

The Wright brothers became interested in flying as kids. In 1878, their father gave them a toy. The boys called it the Bat.

Wilbur and Orville studied how the Bat worked. They played with it until it broke. Then what did they do? Did they throw the Bat away? Not these kids.

They looked at how the toy was put together. Then they built a new one. Then another, and another. Each one was better.

That is how these boys were. They were curious. They wanted to know how things worked.

Wheels and Wings

When they got older, the brothers opened a bike shop. They sold and fixed bikes. They even built bikes of their own. But they never lost their dream of flying.

One day, they saw a photo of Otto Lilienthal. Otto flew **gliders.** A glider is a kind of plane. It has wings but it does not have an engine. Gliders can be hard to control. They rely on the wind.

Otto died in a glider crash. This showed Orville and Wilbur the dangers of flying. They still wanted to try. They planned to build a flying machine. First, they had a lot to learn.

"The Flying Man." *That's what newspapers nicknamed Otto Lilienthal (right). The German engineer made 2,000 glider flights.*

Learning to Fly

Orville and Wilbur studied hard. They read books about flight. They wrote to experts.

They figured out that a flying machine needs three things:

1. It needs **wings** to lift itself into the air. The wings should be curved on top.
2. It needs a source of **power,** such as an engine.
3. It needs **controls** for balance.

Other people had already tested wings and engines. The biggest problem was the controls. Flying an aircraft was hard. A small wind could shake the wings. Then the machine might crash.

Bird Watching

The Wright brothers watched large birds called buzzards. These birds kept balanced by twisting the tips of their wings.

The brothers got an idea. Maybe they could twist, or **warp,** the wings of their plane. It just might work.

Buzzard

Big Day. *Orville Wright's diary (above) is open to December 17, 1903—the date of his historic flight.*

Flying Lessons. *Wilbur Wright pilots a glider in October 1902. This success encouraged the Wrights to build an engine-powered aircraft.*

Kites and Gliders

Wilbur and Orville tested their idea on a kite. They tied strings to the tips of the kite. They pulled the strings for control.

Next, the Wrights built a glider. Making a glider was not easy, though. It took two years to get the design right.

The Right Wings

The Wright brothers tested their first glider in 1900. It stayed in the air for only a short time.

So the Wright brothers got busy. They tried many different wings. They tested many shapes. At last, they found a design that worked. That was in August 1902.

Walking Tall. *Orville (at left) and Wilbur Wright visit a New York air show in 1910. By then the brothers were famous pilots.*

© CORBIS (BOTH)

Making History

Would *Flyer 1* really fly? Orville and Wilbur were ready to find out. They took the plane to Kitty Hawk. But there were problems from the start. Storms kept them on the ground. Then the propellers broke. A month passed.

Finally, the brothers were ready. Wilbur was the first to try the plane. It started to lift into the air. But he pulled too hard on the controls. He crashed into the sand. Repairing the plane took two days.

Now it was Orville's turn. *Flyer 1* lifted up and stayed in the air! The flight lasted only 12 seconds. Yet it made history. *Flyer 1* became the world's first airplane.

Powered Flight

Now Wilbur and Orville were ready for the last big step. They added power. The Wright brothers built their own engine. The engine turned **propellers.** These pushed the plane through the air. Soon, the brothers had their first flying machine. They called it *Flyer 1.*

Wordwise

glider: machine that is like an airplane, but without an engine

propeller: spinning part that pushes a plane through the air

warp: to twist

Flyer 1

Famous photo: The first flight

Flyer 1 did what no aircraft had ever done: By its own power, the plane moved through the air under a pilot's control. This diagram shows key parts of Wilbur and Orville Wright's 1903 invention.

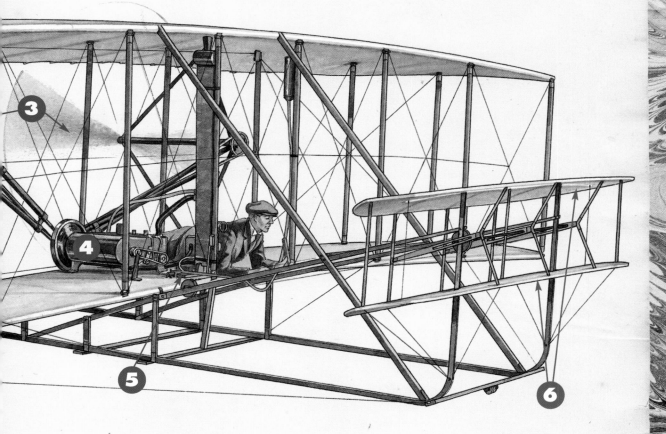

1 **Wing–warping wires**
By pulling the wires, the pilot could move the wing tips—and keep the plane balanced.

2 **Rudders**
Shifting these strips of cloth made the plane turn left or right.

3 **Propellers**
They pushed *Flyer 1* forward.

4 **Engine**
Burning gasoline created power for turning the propellers.

5 **Wing–warping cradle**
The pilot moved his hips to control the wing–warping wires and the rudders.

6 **Elevators**
The position of these small wings made *Flyer 1* move up or down.

DIAGRAM BY JACK MCMASTER FROM FIRST TO FLY, A MADISON PRESS BOOK
PRODUCED FOR CROWN PUBLISHERS; © BETTMANN/CORBIS (PHOTO).

Setting Records. *Earhart smiles after setting a new women's altitude record in 1931.*

Taking Risks. *Earhart looks at a map showing her planned route around the world.*

Amelia Earhart:

What did people say when the Wright brothers tried to fly? "You are crazy! Flying is for birds!"

What did they say when Amelia Earhart tried to fly? "You are crazy! Flying is for boys!"

Earhart proved that women could fly. She became one of the most famous pilots of her day.

Flying High

Earhart learned to fly in the early 1900s. It was a time when most women did not have jobs. And they sure did not fly. But that did not stop Earhart from trying.

She took flying lessons. Then she bought a plane. Soon she made history. In 1932, she flew across the Atlantic Ocean. She was the first woman to do that!

Earhart's flying goggles

Gaining Fame. *Earhart earned great honors in her short life. Here she is cheered after flying alone across the Atlantic in 1932.*

Flying Into Fame

Setting Records

Earhart set many flying records. She flew higher than other women pilots. And farther and faster too.

In 1935, she did something no one had ever done before. She flew alone across the Pacific Ocean.

Her real dream was to fly around the world. In 1937, she set off on her journey. She flew for six weeks. Then something happened.

Around the World

Her plane ran into trouble. People think it crashed. Earhart was never seen again.

She never finished her flight. But she showed that women could be brave. They could take risks. And they could make history.

Earhart's flight helmet

Flight

Answer these questions to find out what you have learned about flight.

1 What got the Wright brothers interested in flying?

2 What was hardest about building a plane?

3 How did buzzards help solve the problem?

4 What was *Flyer 1*?

5 Who was Amelia Earhart? Why is she famous?